FALSE HORIZON

SUE STANDING
FALSE HORIZON

FOUR WAY BOOKS
NEW YORK CITY

Distributed by
University Press
of New England
Hanover and London

Editorial Office
Four Way Books
PO Box 535, Village Station
New York, NY 10014
www.fourwaybooks.com

Library of Congress
Catalog Card Number: 2002108343

ISBN: 1-884800-46-7

Book Design: Brunel
Cover Art: © 1997 Deborah Newey Ferreri, *Picnic and Two Birds*, collection of the author.

This book is manufactured in the United States of America and printed on acid-free paper.

Four Way Books is a division of Friends of Writers, Inc., a Vermont-based not-for-profit organization. We are grateful for the assistance we receive from individual donors and private foundations.

Distributed by University Press of New England, One Court Street, Lebanon, NH 03766.

CONTENTS

These tested Our Horizon –
Then disappeared
As Birds before achieving
A Latitude.

Our Retrospection of Them
A fixed Delight,
But our Anticipation
A Dice – a Doubt –

—Emily Dickinson

I

PALIMPSEST

Love buries these ghost-forms within us.
—Frank Bidart

This poem is a memory trace.
It is late in the world.

Light peels from the ceiling
and rakes the palings of the arcade.

This poem remembers the summer
with its glimmer of possibility.

It remembers the solstice, the equinox,
the festival days, the shepherd's calendar.

It remembers the liminal landscapes,
the technological reliquaries.

It remembers the silence of science,
where memories shift like tectonic plates.

It remembers a gray heron stalking
along the edge of a mere.

It remembers a small house
on the flank of a mountain.

It remembers Bonnard's standing nude
soaping herself by the tub

looking down at her peach-colored flesh
in the room of luminous tiles.

It remembers the way the torso
holds the whole body.

It remembers the way the wings
of the birds whirred over our heads,

the way our faces change as the light
moves across them into the next century.

MOUVANCE

Today was a day of fragments:
one annunciation per beauty.

I walked out into the wrack
of urban roughage

next to the swamps
of tattered pampas grass.

Above the grid, a wing of cloud
created topographies of doubt:

even the broken-off branches
were flowering.

ISLAND HORIZON

Iona

It's a story you've heard before—
all the boys of marriageable age
lost at sea in a storm.

*

In 563, St. Columba was said
to have come here in a coracle
to convert all of Scotland.

I wandered over the sheep paths
past the monastery and up to
the highest point of the island.

From there I could see Fingal's cave
and the green turf above, and the puffins
flicking over the waves like wind-up toys.

*

I have a rough scarf
woven by the wife
of one of the fishermen.

She might have been
the mother of one
of the boys who died

—or of one of the girls
who would have married
one of the boys who died.

THE MAP

All you did
was unfold the map
and then I was inside
the country of desire

You knew this territory
like the back of your hand
because it was
the back of your hand

At first I could not see
the limits of the canton
the topological features
the prehistoric grotto

and had difficulty
walking fast enough
to keep up with you
in this new country

but now I am learning
how to follow the contour lines
almost perfectly
almost without misstep

ARTIFICIAL HORIZON

Thirty-five hundred feet above the earth, I said goodbye
to the heartland with its musk of animals and alfalfa,

to the Coralville Reservoir and its wounded
peregrine falcon with the dusky blue feathers,

to the lattice of pastures interlaced like Celtic spirals,
full of pink-snouted spotted pigs and overflowing corncribs,

to the cemetery with its black angel and tombstones
engraved with contemporary memento mori—

Garfield the cat, a pack of Marlboros, a Corvette—
instead of death's heads and winged cherubs.

We flew farther—saw the golden dome of the Maharishi
levitating and the barges on the Mississippi marking twain.

And hard by my hip, my pilot star, your long fingers
controlled the ailerons, practicing skid and slip,

touch and go, bank and stall, keeping a steady hand
as we flew beyond the bounds of the artificial horizon.

SEXUAL HORIZON

Prevailing winds. Drama of small gestures.
Light like fine mica falling from the sky.

Your body, my body. We shadow the plot lines.
The square square miles. Water rising.

Artificial flowers glitter like confetti
on the green and gray graves.

A small, plum-colored stain where passion was.
From the air, I can't fathom the flattened

topography, get the bends from too much
air and space, too many cardinal directions.

Like breaking open the corms of irises.
And turn into something someone else would love.

ACCIDENTAL

. . . a fluke in a flock of predictable migrants.
—Terry Tempest Williams

Season of myths and forgetfulness:
I wish I knew these birds by song.

We're on the coast of somewhere,
operating in anecdotal mode.

That must have been then,
but this is now—

no wingspan, no fuel, no lift.
People you didn't know are dying.

THE AVIARY

for Kendra Kopelke

The aviary is disappointing, perhaps—
too much diorama, not enough habitat—
but you would like the hyacinth macaw,
the paradise whydah, and the fairy bluebird,
for their names, if nothing else.

I watch the great hornbill: his yellow casque
shaped like two wooden bananas
hammered together by an inept carpenter;
his eyelashes—tiny feathers, really—
blinking over round, brown humanoid eyes.

He regurgitates bits of lizard and grape
from his long, curved ivory beak
into his mate's equally sculptural maw,
the only thing you can see of her
as she gestates in the mudded-up hollow of a tree.

He makes me want someone
to feed me salmon and melon
while I wait for the world outside
the world inside to do its messy work.

LIFE LIST

The list was dangerous.
It had webbed feet.

The birds arrive in a blur
from over the border.

They drive light from me.
Let me see all of him—

love in the dress of sleep.
After bed, we wanted rain.

Behind us, the garden
could shine on in want.

Unsay it. Gainsay it.
You were never there.

I always make
the same mistake twice.

TOUR D'HORIZON

Here's a path that knows nothing
beyond grim invisibility

a plaque with a stiff inscription
that vanishes in the light

a patch of fluorescent yellow
where there was a planet yesterday

a perfume made of coal and tar
that singes the skin

This is why the ruins
have been made portable

why I hate seascapes
with their moons shadowed on water

why the birds scatter
with a flapping as of broken blinds

why I need a life
that won't tarnish at dusk

SUBURBAN HORIZON

I return to the suburbs of my childhood,
bringing my lover.

Perhaps the dark won't strip the bark
from my limbs this time.

But it's as if snow
has fallen over my whole life.

An exhausted wash of cloud
slews across the sky like a telescope.

When he says "I love you,"
I have to hold the words

up to the light
to look for the watermark.

UNTRANSLATED

The syntactical hinge on which her life depends,
like a landscape in a foreign language.

She longs to be more discursive, but longing
is otherwise. A darkening mirror.

Even the most conventional people need our pity
say the lovers your flesh is heir to.

She had—has—a hard time using things up:
the weight of a word, the graven images.

It was the idea of opera that appealed to her,
unspeakable arias, a wound gone instantly to scar.

She has lost track again. I am alone with her voice
in the woods, a voice that erases pallor.

It wasn't a dream: the car covered with blood
when we turned a corner in the Combat Zone.

A man wiping the blood from his car with his hands,
one boot in the middle of the street, the body gone.

AMOR FATI

What will contain me?
Not this amphora in the shape of a woman's head
nor that vial in the form of a swimmer.
Not these votive objects—hands feet breasts uteri—
nor the incised bronze mirrors
which once held the beauty and sorrows of women.
Not any of these perfumed souvenirs
of the afterworld.

Not even the *sposi,* reclining on their tomb,
voluptuous, entwined, flickering smiles
on their faces, as if what death holds for them—
held for them—is pleasure, which is what
all the perfect Greek sculpture in the world
does not promise the way the Etruscans promise.

Even if love
could be drawn again from their mouths,
it would not be enough to hold us here.
But what else do I have to give you
in this fading light?

(Villa Giulia, XIV April MCMXCII)

IN THE FORUM

Nothing will make us present tense.
Like an agora with nothing to sell,
the past gives up its chips of marble,
broken pediments, headless statues.
No way of knowing whether the fragments
are put together right,
but the forms the particles take

give shape to shapeless lives like our own.
The risks we're taking aren't really risks.
Orange trees. Umbrella pines. Wisteria.
A drift of nuns and schoolchildren.
A scattering of pensioners who get in free.
We look down into the Circus Maximus,
emptied of almost all its obelisks.

From the Farnese gardens, we descend
into the House of Livia—
the painted walls so chicly decomposed
a stage designer would kill for that effect.
A drama of betrayal would be perfect
set against that fractured sky—
love stretched thinner than a wishbone.

SICILIAN VESPERS

It was raining all over Sicily. We couldn't see
anything from Enna or Taormina. It was so dark
we had to keep putting coins in the meters

at the cathedrals to see the mosaics.
This is all I remember about Palermo:
niches with candles and statues of the virgin,

the orange trees in the ruined cloister,
the artichokes we bought from huge pots
of boiling water at the market and carried back

to our room-without-a-view in Monreale.
This is all I remember: driving down the tiled
cathedral steps in Caltigirone, because I couldn't

find the café where you were waiting out of the rain.
Che brutto tempo! Che brutto tempo! the shopkeepers said.
What foul moods we both were in. Wet clothes and flat tires.

Greek ruins in the rain.
Your ancestors' hill town in the rain.
Everything in the rain.

Your face in the rain.

II

EVENT HORIZON

What Brownian motion set us spinning so near the brink
of each other.

"We was dazed. We was confused. We didn't know
what we hit."

He misread her handwriting, deciphering "oracles"
as "octaves."

At the Precision Museum, a woman calls her lover
from a pay phone.

"Why can we remember the past but not
the future?"

She hoped their love would not prove fugitive
to light.

"How quickly these accidents happen, and then one returns
to the old life." "I don't."

THE ART OF SWIMMING

One may attain to the art of swimming perfectly.

Listen, I'll tell you how it feels
to be underwater all the time.
Afternoon leaps from my thighs;
the sun splits everything into fibers.

As a rule, women learn to float more quickly
than men, because their bones are lighter.
Few male swimmers can float in fresh water at all.

In the water field. This place is mine
and the snapping turtle's. Bluebottles
and dragonflies form a halo around me as I limn
the water and gather my flotilla of bones.

There is nothing more fascinating to a swimmer
than a sharp, clean plunge into cool water.

Like a homing pigeon, I return to the pool
and enter the water, messages tied to my fingers
and toes, messages released as I swim. Sighs span
out on each breath, enough to carry me a mile.

He that learns to Swim ought to have his Animal
Spirits at perfect liberty and command.

Water slides over my collarbone like silk.
Under your hands, I'm all sinew, the little mermaid.
No shadow trails me; I must swim or die,
a knifethrower's kiss on the template of the body.

There is no season wherein a man may not have
the occasion to practice the Art of Swimming;
but any season is not proper to learn it in.

One winter, the swimming pool freezes: a glacier,
a jade-colored mountain in the backyard. Inside,
there are semi-precious stones: milky opals,
ziggurats of topaz, a heart of palest aquamarine.

The first general consideration in such a Theory
ought to be the Specific or Comparative Weight of Bodies
in the respective fluids designed to practice in.

Swimming in the fast lane, I'm Perpetua. In my end
is my beginning, the pool a Möbius strip: strange loops,
bounded loops, free loops. I swim in a current of numbers,
two sevens attached to my shoulders like waterwings.

If there be only slight breathing, or no breathing,
or if the breathing fail, then, to excite breathing
turn the patient well and instantly on the side,
supporting the head, and excite the nostrils with snuff,
hartshorn, and smelling-salts, or tickle the throat
with a feather, etc., if they are at hand.

On a dipsomaniac night when the wind encounters
a starfish twice its size—so deciduously graceful
each motion collapses before it begins—dredged
and scattered pieces of water barnacle our bodies.

One may attain to the habit of swimming perfectly.

SOLITAIRE

The Venerable Bede was here & here
thanks to the prick of the needle
of his temperament & faith.

Now, at Jarrow, in a vacant lot
near the ruins of his monastery
& the window made from fragments
of the oldest stained glass in England,
we see a huge hoarding
announcing "Bede's World":

What will it be?
An Anglo-Saxon Disneyland
of Viking raids & blown-up runes?
Battery-powered anchorites & cutaway
views of an abbey like an antfarm?
Or a library of writhing scribes,
tonsured & humming in the secrecy
of their solitude tunes no one
has heard for twelve hundred years?

Drawn to the eremitical & the ruined,
I discover that loneliness is random,
solitude ritual.
And scribal error is rampant.
"God should not be subject
to the Art of Grammar,"
wrote your abbot Aelfric
in one of his prefaces.

But whose naked narrative will suffice?
"These admonitions are suitable for the teachable;
for the unteachable & hard of heart
no encouragements are sufficient."

This is your world now, not Bede's,
& I am becoming familiar
with what bones of it are left—

from the pagan thrill of Cerne Abbas,
priapic giant cheek by jowl
with the spell of Augustine's well;
to the pillow stones at Lindisfarne,
with their uneven quadrants
of crosses & names & runes;
to the uncorrupted body
of St. Cuthbert at Durham—

all embedded in the privacy
of a stopped tongue,
the solitary unravelling
of the scholar.

FIVE RIDDLES

1.

Maze, flytrap, sticky lair
for the tongue's honey,
my labyrinthine corridors hold
more than you can imagine—
blacksmith's tools or symphony.

2.

Bag of bones, nest of nerves,
I flush or freeze, shake or shiver.
Warren of wiggle, I self-repair
my host of curves.

3.

Choose: backward or forward.
You can use me,
but you can't use me up.

4.

Creature of paradox:
once I was soft as skin,
now hard as bedrock.
My heart of flint
can be sparked with a tap.
Then I emerge like the map
of an unknown country:
embedded until you see me.

5.

Come closer, listen to this
echo of ancient oracles, these
layers of murmuring melodies.
Listen to my voice—
open me, open my cup of sound.

LAPSES

It will take more than Smokey
& The Miracles or The Temptations
to get me out of bed this morning.

We made love like two radio wave-
lengths colliding between cities;
like explorers finding islands

lost on all nautical charts;
parachute silk and artificial tears
seeding a low-to-the-ground virga.

Who are you anyway?
—the sweet angel of midnight lust
or the terrible egoist of daylight?

Are you a planetary luminary,
or merely post-solstice light
with crescent moon shoulder blades?

If I could penetrate your life
unseen, like a clothes-moth burning
a nearly-invisible aperture,

then I could lie in the winter light
and listen to church bells,
a keeper of wishful ideas.

THE GOOD LIFE

seems to include lots of fake animals
scattered around the yard.

Somewhere (I know where) American families
are still dining in their cars.

A carhop waits on them, brings the food,
and attaches it to a tray on the window.

The news is frivolous today—
some guy who wants his antlers back,

and a religious freedom case:
"God and the Internal Revenue Service

have nothing in common with each other
and don't really understand each other."

The good life breezes by the grafted tree
without looking back, and the suburbanites

put up their Malthus wallpaper, a soothing
pattern of peas and bunnies multiplying.

Some people would be perfectly happy
in a universe where things had no names.

The good life lives in the past
because there's no future there.

SHRINE

What is not obvious
is not obvious to me.

Things happen in time,
but history passes

into implausibility.
Here, for example,

is a kind of casino of faith
full of generic nativity scenes:

Indian, Eskimo, African.
Among these pasteboard

representations of the divine,
the unlined countenances

of the faithful
are counterpoised

against the deep lines
on the skeptic's brow.

Instead, I want a pure dark
shock of pagan winter pain.

URBAN HORIZON

Bitter city I can't find
the juice of you any more,

only the pith and unwashed flesh.
Past the disembodied,

the mumbling, those whose gestures
mirror my own. *Want, Don't Want*,

the crosswalk signal says.
I'm taking the risk

of finding you alone and awake,
or at least not not alone.

INVISIBLE HORIZON

Where I came from it was cloudy
and I couldn't see the mountains

When I call, you tell me
your weather is better than mine

I want a house-shaped house
with a view of a river

in listening distance
of train whistles or foghorns

Other people won't stay
where we put them

Someone takes care of the roses
but not of me

In moonlight I can see the shadow
of a tree that is no longer there

URBAN THRUSH

A bird I've never heard before.
Because you're not here,
I make everything a sign,

this song the sign
that you might come to love
this clamorous place the way I do.

HUMMINGBIRD

No matter how fast my heart,
yours beats faster.

What would ever
make you stay?

A rose named for Frédéric Mistral.
The Arctic Queen Nectarine.

Orchids in Malawi
(over four hundred species).

Kashmiri meadows
might keep you

for more than a
millisecond touch-and-go.

Yours beats faster,
no matter how fast my heart.

VIEW

Today the bay's a faded tablecloth,
no wrinkles on the lost horizon.

It always comes down to this:
a room, a table, paper and pencil.

And at night the beam of the lighthouse
like a punctuating cyclops.

Everything stripped down to sky, sea—
some days, no sky, no sea,

only fog like a theatrical scrim
promising riches when it rises.

WATER GARDEN

Lotus sliced flat against
the black impasto of the page,

lung-shaped leaves like
a palm-print shadowing

the palpable undercurrent.
Above this latitude of lassitude,

you cannot see the fountain,
a bronze boy holding a seahorse.

You cannot see
the cynosure of love, or doubt.

LATE SUMMER ELEGY

in memory of Harvey Oxenhorn

Today the Mt. San Angelo barn looks fixed in ruin,
the timbre of thunder displacing the roosters
that crow all day announcing life and life and life.

The persistent sculptor a neighbor calls "the peckerwood"
rhythmically chips at her limestone plinth.
Your death follows me through landscapes you loved,

past pink thistles on which bees impale themselves
and swallowtails pumping up pollen like oil
as they fan slow vees in the air with their wings.

Earlier this summer, so soon after you died,
it followed me past that rice paddy in Tanzania—
where, in memory, white ibises rose all at once.

When my long thighs strained to carry me up the slippery scree
at the edge of the gorge, I felt you: *Go on, don't hold back.*
This wind touches your face now, then is gone.

And when I wanted—no, too expensive, I cannot eat them—
those purple anemones in the market, I heard: *Desire.*
Like a phrase of Brahms played over and over.

In a postcard you sent from Greenland, you wrote
how you watched your *Regina Maris* shipmates butcher
a seventy-five-pound halibut, how you held its heart, still beating.

Now, you sail farther, into northern light.

YASHODA AND KRISHNA

Your almond eyes are shut. He presses
your right nipple while sucking your left.

I, too, have peeled the spiky rind
and eaten the plush flesh:

Take, eat of this fruit.

Before the sky was quite light,
you stepped into the hot springs

and smoothed the heavy mineral water—
dark as the skin of a plum—over your thighs.

How did you learn to leave him?

I had too many dreams of drowning
and the bees began to swarm.

SOLSTICE, BLUE MOUNTAIN LAKE

Here, woods threaded
by knock and chush and tick

here, delicate wild irises
my mother would have loved

here, a hermit thrush
I take as mine

here, bear scat
and coyote track

here in the dusky meadow,
deer, unafraid

and at water's edge
to mark the solstice, here

miniature birchbark rafts
are launched with a cargo

of candles that glimmer
briefly like fireflies

before they sink
into the dark lake,

the echo of loon calls

PERMISSIVE PATH

The thought "as if."
She remembers the line

of cypresses
spelling "cemetery."

She has become chary of pleasure,
charred by desire.

No punishment is necessary
or desirable.

She refuses to think about angels,
even the sad angel

of the breakfast table
who reproaches her each morning.

They have reached the borderline
of musical hysteria.

She sees things more clearly
if someone else describes.

NOVEMBER HORIZON

Not even a weather-glim to redeem
this bleak day. It's been twenty years.

Grief is endless and invisible,
grief is signifier to the word:

a fountain, a dry stone wall,
an electric fence you can't let go of.

My name is I-want-to-believe
and my doubt is legion.

I exist in these words like shadow, bread,
something soldering the heart.

FLESH DRESS

La chair est triste, hélas! et j'ai lu tous les livres.
—Stéphane Mallarmé

I wanted to become a new person,
not someone who lived in an unhappy body

like a star-nosed mole.
So I tried protective coloration:

in a field of broken-down sunflowers,
I became the most bowed, the spikiest;

in a bar I became the drunkest,
the one who danced the longest;

in the water I became the reflection
no light could shine through.

But since I couldn't erase myself,
I became myself,

flayed and open to the world—
no bones, only flesh and restlessness.

WATER LEVEL

for Katherine Kadish

I never thought I'd want the past again—
those unlyric shapes, unholy patterns

of linoleum squares, metal tumblers,
chrome & vinyl, scarred Formica.

Everything there was hooked, torn,
grafted, quilted, under the fluorescent

middle-of-the-century light.
It was a world like a rough, green apple

where fathers spoke only to ask
when the food would be on the table.

But yesterday in the buoyant waters
of the mineral baths at Warm Springs,

as we floated among the islands of other women
in our spa-issued rompers of gingham & rickrack—

something—the feel of the billowing cloth?
the vivid triangle of your uplifted chin?—

made me think I might go back after all,
as if into an old lake's amber water.

BLAZON

Your hair of egret feathers
Your eyes of sea almonds

Your ears without names
Your lips of lightning flashes

Your tongue of calla lilies
Your arms of divining rods

Your hands of palm fronds
Your nipples of pomegranate seeds

Your navel of whirlwinds
Your sex of rivers

Your thighs of igneous rock
Your knees of proverbs

Your calves, your feet

FLAMBOYAN

for David Green

A scent of moss or humus—
as if you had just come
from a greenhouse
full of birds of paradise,
lilies and orchids.

Your eyes—clear as beryl
from Minas Gerais—
speak of water and sun.
Your hands stroke my shoulder,
speak Spanish
even when your voice
of lavish honey does not.

Half your life ago, a moment
caught you—joyful, naked—
in a waterfall.
Now, as you cover me
with starfish kisses,
the cascade's inside me—
flamboyan, red as a heart.

III

CARPE DIEM

I had gone to the museum for cautionary reasons,
for:
        memento mori
        martyrs
        the weeping at the tomb
        saints translated into heaven

but all the women in portraits looked as if they were
        contemplating sleeping with the painter

They all looked guilty of something

Even the virgin seemed to be gazing lustfully
        at the baby Jesus

Skin is skin when your own limbs are electric

Painted flesh like ripe fruit

A cut pomegranate like the inside of desire

The stems of the lilies troubled with dew

Only Preti's *Prophète*—his hand upraised
        in a warning gesture, his holy book open
        to the relevant scriptural passage—
        struck the proper apocalyptic note I was looking for

Of Prudence, Love, and Grace,
        I was trying to identify with Prudence

I wanted the cooling marble of neoclassic
        but I got Leda & the Swan
        in a particularly heated moment

Then everything narrowed to a few manacles of light

I saw myself as in a baroque mirror, gilt edges,
        a wavering image

And I knew what it was like to be in the world again,
        flung into the fine ache of longing

ALBA

If the morning could keep this frieze
of rumpled sheets like fossil imprints
in the lumpy bed, then I might also
keep the hawk over the ravine, the flawed
image in the mirror, the new wine.

Last night in the empty vineyards
I looked west to the fast-moving clouds
over Rocher des Vierges, and I wanted to hold that.
And hold the silence—or almost silence—
broken by a few barking dogs and the sound
of the seedpods shaking on the plane tree.

Impossible to keep anything. Impossible
to carry anything away, at least
not what I want to take: fistfuls
of flowering herbs, the wind from any
of the six directions, love's progress—
if, that is, it's possible for love
to progress, when it may be rooted
like local honey in the *domaine*
with the stubborn vines, among the strong
flavors of this world, rose garlic, *aneth,*
black radishes—and you, this morning.

MONTPEYROUX

On one side of the mountain, wildness—
thorn trees, gorse, wild herbs,
and rock formations
honeycombed by wind.

On the other, cultivation—
roads and ditches, villages and vineyards,
each *domaine* a different color and shape
with variant ways of stringing the vines.

The stumps of old vines
are knotted and ventricular like hearts,
or staked out like the tortured
crucifixes in the village churches,

where clusters of grapes
twining up the columns
are more than metaphorical,
here where wine is blood.

Balanced on the ramparts
of the ruined castle,
we feel the zigzagging walls
are fragile as if "out of paper pared."

The wind—it could be *mistral, tramontane,*
or one of thirty other sorts—
blows so hard that dried pods
rattle like maracas, and raptors
stay suspended in one spot.

From up here, we can almost see
the *étangs* of the Mediterranean

with their improbable flamingoes
that migrate all the way
from Lake Nakuru in Kenya.

Closer, moving along an irrigation ditch,
is a horse tied by a rope to a car—
out for an evening stroll?
In the village, a yellow-and-blue
tent's set up for the carnival:
"Cirque Jackson," the posters read.

Outside the tent, men—red-faced, worn-looking—
smoke, waiting for the women
and children to emerge. The tent
is so small that inside must be
miniature equestriennes and secret
small elephants and tigers.

Soon we will go down, past the plane tree
to which twenty hooves are nailed,
past the tobacconist's, the bakery,
the solid houses with doors like coffin lids.

The wind will sweep us through Rue de la Dysse,
and into the cold stone room
where we will drink strong *vin de pays,*
eat wild asparagus,

and speak of the particular names
made for this landscape—
garrigue, maquis, bories—
their thorny syllables
impossible to translate.

ABOVE TAÜLL

The air smelled different without him—
around him he had always carried
a scent of honey and rosemary,
of possibility and aerial views.

Above Taüll, she climbed on sheep trails,
avoiding the thorny scrub full of thistles and allium.
It was midday. She'd breakfasted on churros and coffee,
brought cheese and pears to eat on the mountain.

Now the compass seemed off,
the strata shifted, the river
running in the wrong direction.
Perhaps she has lost herself in loss.

The tourists were elsewhere.
She took off her clothes. She wanted to sleep until
she entered the local, the unnamed, until
she could hear nothing but the dull clank of sheepbells.

From the two Romanesque churches,
bells struck, out of phase, wavering
with the distance—the whole valley
beneath her, nothing much in it.

OUR LADY OF THE ASSUMPTION

Without knowing it,
I had opened
my hand to him
for the last time,
entered a world
indecipherable
as his handwriting.

Until now,
I thought travel
was a metaphor
for sleep, thought ice
was the equivalent
of silence, thought
after was after all.

Master of Cabestany,
I trace your capitals,
I ask for a sign.
In the stairwell
to the martyrs,
I find a scrap of paper—
one line is legible.

CLOISTER

Now it is evening
and the lyric sublime has shut up.

Stripped down to purest Romanesque,
I'm waiting for the eleventh-century sun

to spiral down the naked columns
inside St. Guilhem-le-Désert.

On the Hudson, where you are,
are all the missing pieces, all the riches:

arcade and garden,
gilt and polychrome,

the pilfered capitals and carvings
reconstructed in twentieth-century niches.

We started like a romance,
and ended like a religious tract—

twin saints in an infirmary of stars,
blue xenon colliding with red neon.

Amazing how unattractive
skepticism can be,

as ugly as the one true thing left here,
a reliquary holding finger bones.

If I could pray or beget, if I could leave
the cold shadow and enter. . . .

It’s lonely here, without a doubt,
and there’s more company in belief.

BOUNDED

Inside *l'atelier d'architecture,*
a woman bends over her blueprints.

Le bonheur est fait avec de petit petit bonheur.
A room inside a room inside a room.

A woman bends over her blueprints—
a plain room for dreaming,

a room inside a room inside a room—
with her T-square, her compass.

A plain room for dreaming,
and outside the windows a mackerel sky.

With her T-square, her compass,
she praises the makers of cairns, of tumuli.

And outside the windows a mackerel sky.
A woman's body is a house

praising the makers of cairns, of tumuli.
If she could see inside, she could remember

that a woman's body is a house.
She could remember where she has been

if she could see inside; she could remember
her own happiness.

She could remember where she has been:
Le bonheur est fait avec de petit petit bonheur,

her own happiness
inside *l'atelier d'architecture*.

FALSE HORIZON

Is this the same road or a different road?
Not so much translated as transposed.

What else would have made the flowers
lose their color so suddenly?

Maybe time has passed.
They call it continuity.

You've been here, but it looks like
somewhere you've never been.

Don't suffer yourself so much:
the place you thought this was

has become a habit the same as another,
one you inhabit like a drafty room.

An hour of this, an hour of that:
then silence.

What is true is not probable;
what is probable is not true.

THE VILLAGE

I. Guided Tour

"Follow your nose," the guidebook says,
to the only active cowshed in a *bastide* village.
And it's true M. Roget is out at all hours
trucking cow dung from the shed to his fields,
prodding the cows for a walkabout,
or bringing up some fragrant new hay.
He's the only farmer left in this village—
some kind of *droit de seigneur*—
but he's a nocturnal farmer.
All night, you can hear the loud *beep beep beep*
as his tractor backs up onto the Place de la République
(a grand name for such a small square),
narrowly missing the stone pillar on which
is mounted a wood and metal crucifix.
Tripod, the three-legged, one-eyed
pregnant cat might be what you notice next.
She's popular with the local toms
by which she's birthed at least half the cats in town.
If it's laundry day, you'll smell soap
and bluing and bleach or trip over the rows
of linens hung to dry in the narrow streets
next to the profusion of geraniums, impatiens,
and oleanders on every step, windowsill and curb.
It seems a kind of competition
among the local madames, to see who
can be most picturesque and drown
the smell of M. Roget's cows.

II. The Store

I stay in; I mind my business,
I know I don't belong—
don't know when to open or shut my shutters,
when to hang out the laundry,
or when it's proper to appear in public
with *poubelle* sac in hand.
And each day when I work up the courage
to go to the *alimentation,*
the proprietress—plump, blonde,
made-up and overripe,
playing the part of a shopkeeper
in the style of Fellini, not Truffaut—
doesn't know what to do with me,
whether to call me "Mlle" or "Mme,"
or how much French I actually understand.
She's all bustle and push,
as if impatient to get off the movie set
and to the back lot for a cigarette.
"Bonjour, les filles," she calls out theatrically
to a small troupe of girls coming for ice cream.
No problem there. But she looks at me crossly
when I pick up a baguette so I don't know
whether I can pick up a small pyramid of *cabecou*
or touch the *pêches, pommes,* or *abricots*
that her husband, who's nicer,
but never works the till,
arranges in crates by the door
near stacks of long-life milk.
All summer long I try to make her smile,

a little crack in her pancake facade—
when I buy every cleaning product in the store,
when I say I've never tasted such fine melons,
when I ask for something and mangle the name—
but she keeps slowly counting out my change,
putting it on the scale, not in my outstretched hand,
and looking off into the middle distance, waiting for action.

III. Unsent Postcard from the Porte de l'irrisou

My dearest Hedgehog,
did you know that *irrisou*
is Occitan for hedgehog?
Today I wandered around the ramparts . . .

IV. Midi, après-midi

Now, when the Angelus peals, it seems
that bits of language like potsherds
assemble themselves into a vessel
even the *mistral* can't penetrate,
however strongly it blows and bruises
almond blossoms, lavender, iris, and
narcisse des poètes—six white petals
with *une odeur suave,* my guidebook says.
In such a moment, it does no good
to long for something different,
though longing makes us unfold

and rearrange this cloud of unknowing,
outside of time, against the sky of history.

V. La fête

I pass two slow trucks that read *Bal musette,*
no doubt on their way to another village fête—
sanglier in Montmiral or oysters at Sête.
Ours was last month in the *place* where we met.
Something you wanted that you didn't get—
like the prizes at the *pêche aux canards* set
up for the children while their elders stepped
lively, sambas and rhumbas in them yet.
Some old farm couples, up since dawn, slept
at the tables while the accordians wept.
I got tired of asking: *Est-tu prête?*
What if you had actually placed your bet
so now you'd not be flirting with regret?
Qui sème le vent récolte la tempête.

VI. Boules

Heavy clack of the petanque balls squiffing earth.
Voices rising from under the lindens
on the esplanade toward my monastic window.
Doucement, doucement, one of them says.
Précisément, another I recognize as the mayor replies.

"I am not going to rob myself of my own happiness,"
Susan's aunt wrote after her fiancé died in the Great War.
And I must try not to rob myself of mine, I think,
as I go out to walk in the long twilight.

VII. Poème péage

Vent violent,
soyez prudent.

VIII. Le film

My last morning in the village.
I walk over to the *place* to make a phone call.
Everything has been rearranged—
the school is vine-covered
and sporting a huge sign, *Auberge du Causse,*
over green umbrellas and café chairs.
The *alimentation* is *Boutique Margo.*
The *real* café is now *La Poste.*
La Poste is nowhere to be found.
Will the telephone box
still hold a telephone?
I make my call and walk back through
what turns out to be a set for a *téléfilm:*
La Causse d'Aspignac.
It looks like a real village,
but it's not my village.

What if they had made a film of us
when we still looked like a couple?

IX. La canicule

Flash! The butcher has closed
and M. Roget has sold his cows
(no connection between the two events),
so there's no more *beep beep beep*
of Roget's tractor backing up
in the middle of the night as he herds.
He's kept one mean-tempered one, though,
which he douses with a disinfectant
that reeks of coal tar & gasoline.
Also, for the first time ever,
he has put flowers outside his house—
true, they are in white plastic dishpans
atop old tires, but they *are* flowers—
impatiens and petunias.
During the height of mad cow madness,
he put up a sign on his stable door:
SI LES VACHES
IMPORTUNE LA
POPULACE
LA MUNICIPALITÉ
DOIT M'INDEMNISER
PRIX 3000000,00F (trois cent mille francs).
And Jasmin, a.k.a. Tripod, has had
another litter of kittens.

X. Beyond the Porte d'irrisou

Below the house with blue shutters,
below the ramparts,
onto the sheep path through the sloes,
past the disused communal bathing cistern,
through the orchard of specimen trees—
mirabelle, cerise, abricot, pêche—
and into the oak woods where the path divides:
petit sentier or *grande randonée* this morning?
Down to the glade to the trickle I call Hölderlin's waterfall
or up to the fire lookout high in the Grésigne?

Song of blackbird, flash of goldfinch,
I want to follow that hawk and be lifted.

THE HORIZON OF INEXHAUSTIBLE IDEALITY

Why don't places remember people?
The images leak through

a crack in the dark,
with a fetch of southerly wind.

Small bronze butterflies
light on the fallen plums.

We were driven out of paradise,
but paradise remained intact.

You wanted a waterfall so here
is this cool and delicious runnel.

Hölderlin's pollen could not
be more yellow or more fine.

The names are so perfect
the flowers are unnecessary.

ACKNOWLEDGMENTS

My thanks to the editors of the following publications in which these poems firs appeared, some in slightly different versions:

Agni	Palimpsest
The American Scholar	In the Forum
Atlanta Review	Five Riddles
The Atlantic Monthly	Hummingbird
Boston Review	Montpeyroux
Compost	The Art of Swimming
	The Good Life
Denver Quarterly	Our Lady of the Assumption
Greensboro Review	Amor Fati
	Bounded
Harvard Review	Event Horizon
The Iowa Review	Alba
	Flamboyan
	The Horizon of Inexhaustible Ideality
The Journal	Untranslated
lyric	Blazon
	The Map
Marlboro Review	Artificial Horizon
Oregon Review	Carpe Diem
Orion	Accidental
	The Aviary
Partisan Review	Solitaire
PersePhonic	Permissive Path
	Sexual Horizon
Runes	Flesh Dress
Poetry 2000 Desk Calendar	View
	Water Garden
Salamander	Invisible Horizon
Southwest Review	Water Level
Sou'wester	November Horizon
	Suburban Horizon
Urban Nature	Mouvance

Many of these poems also appeared in *The Cape Split Cycle* exhibition catalog, produced by the Virginia Museum of Fine Arts.

"Alba," "Palimpsest," and "Mouvance" are recorded on the CD *One Side of the River: Poets of Cambridge & Somerville* from Say That! Productions.

The other epigraphs in the book are taken from the following sources:

Frank Bidart, "Thinking Through Form" in *Ecstatic Occasions, Expedient Forms*, 2nd ed., ed. David Lehman (Ann Arbor: University of Michigan Press, 1996).

Stéphane Mallarmé, "Brise marine" in *Poésies* (Paris: Gallimard, 1952).

Terry Tempest Williams, *Refuge* (New York: Vintage, 1992).

I am grateful to the Corporation of Yaddo, Hawthornden Castle, the MacDowell Colony, the Massachusetts Cultural Council, the Virginia Center for the Creative Arts, and Wheaton College for time and space in which to work. My gratitude also to Katherine Kadish and Eileen Mott for their work on *The Cape Split Cycle*, to Deborah Newey Ferreri for her permission to reproduce *Picnic and Two Birds*, and to David Barber, Teresa Cader, Steven Cramer, David Green, Alice Hoffman, Kendra Kopelke, Joyce Peseroff, Martha Rhodes, and Stephen Tapscott for their support and advice throughout.

Sue Standing's previous books of poetry include *Amphibious Weather, Deception Pass,* and *Gravida*. She is the recipient of several grants, including residencies from Hawthornden Castle, the MacDowell Colony, the Virginia Center for the Creative Arts, and the Corporation of Yaddo, and fellowships from the National Endowment for the Arts and the Bunting Institute of Radcliffe College. She is Professor of English at Wheaton College (Norton, Massachusetts), where she directs the Creative Writing Program.